The New Novello Choral Edition

CHARLES GOUNOD

Messe solennelle de Sainte Cécile

for soprano, tenor and bass solists, SATB and orchestra or organ and/or piano *ad lib.*

Revised by Michael Pilkington

ISBN: 978-0-85360-980-3

NOVELLO

part of **WiseMusic***Group*

EXCLUSIVELY DISTRIBUTED BY
HAL•LEONARD®

Visit Hal Leonard Online at
www.halleonard.com

Contact us:
Hal Leonard
7777 West Bluemound Road
Milwaukee, WI 53213
Email: info@halleonard.com

In Europe, contact:
Hal Leonard Europe Limited
42 Wigmore Street
Marylebone, London, W1U 2RY
Email: info@halleonardeurope.com

In Australia, contact:
Hal Leonard Australia Pty. Ltd.
4 Lentara Court
Cheltenham, Victoria, 3192 Australia
Email: info@halleonard.com.au

It is requested that on all concert notices and programmes acknowledgement is made to 'The New Novello Choral Edition'.
Es wird gebeten, auf sämtlichen Konzertankündigungen und Programmen 'The New Novello Choral Edition' als Quelle zu erwähnen.
Il est exigé que toutes les notices et programmes de concerts, comportent des remerciements à 'The New Novello Choral Edition'.

Orchestral material is available for hire from the publishers

Cover illustration: first vocal entry in the 'Kyrie eleison' of Gounod's *Messe Solennelle de Sainte Cécile* from Lebeau's 1879 edition.

Preface

Gounod's *Messe solennelle de Sainte Cécile* was first performed on St Cecilia's Day, 22 November 1855, and the full score was published by Lebeau the same year. It was reissued in 1865. In 1870 Novello published a vocal score with an organ accompaniment arranged by Joseph Barnby. In 1874 Goddard & Co. issued a vocal score with the following introductory note by the composer:

TO THE MUSICAL PUBLIC

This Mass (St Cecilia) was written in the year 1853 (twenty years ago).

I discovered last year that it had not been properly protected at Stationers' Hall, and that the great English publishing firms had not scrupled to publish it, solely for their own benefit, not only in almost the original form but cut up, made into pieces for the organ, and adapted to the Protestant form of worship. This I strongly object to - uselessly, I am aware, as it is a time-honoured practice in England.

I have, however, been persuaded by many friends to write an Organ Accompaniment and a second Offertory for the Mass, as this expedient, I am informed, in a small measure restores to me my lost property.

I have, therefore, not hesitated to use what, *in my hands*, are, I believe, legitimate means for the purposes of recovering some of those rights in this work, of which, as in the case of so many other works, I have been deprived by the licence which the laxity of the law allows the vigilant cupidity of the musical trade.

CH. GOUNOD
Tavistock House, Tavistock Square
December, 1873.

In 1879 Lebeau published this new organ arrangement by the composer without the second Offertory. In 1880 Novello published a vocal score with an accompaniment arranged for piano by Barnby, the edition that this revision supercedes. In line with Lebeau, the second Offertory has not been included in this revised edition.

The 1874 edition has the accompaniment laid out on two and, where pedal notes are required, three staves. Despite the fact that Gounod stated that he had made an organ accompaniment for this edition, some of the passages on two staves frequently employ notes below the range of the organ keyboard. This, together with the 'una corda' pedalling instructions and separate staves for the harp on pages 46-51, and the fact that in the 1874 edition the *Invocation* [Offertory] was arranged for piano duet, makes it obvious that Gounod assumed the presence of piano as well as organ.

The passages on three staves that include pedal notes, and are therefore definitely intended for the organ are as follows:

- Kyrie
- Gloria, bb.1-37
- Credo, bb.85-100; 253 (by implication 242)-260, where the four stave layout implies the lower two staves are organ to the end
- Offertory, arranged for piano duet in 1874, for organ solo in 1879; Barnby's piano duet version could be used if desired
- Sanctus
- Benedictus, although on two staves the registration indicates this was intended for organ
- Agnus Dei, bb.8-16, 26-36, 44-end

The 1879 edition removed most of the notes below low C shown in Gounod's original vocal score in the two stave sections. These have been restored for use at the piano, but in small print for the benefit of organists. It would seem possible to arrange a very satisfactory performance with judicious use of both piano and organ. Dynamic indications in square brackets and slurs and hairpins with strokes are taken from the full score of 1855.

Further points to note:

For the chorus the original heading 'Soprano II', normal in French scores, has been changed to Alto, normal in most other countries.

Gloria in excelsis, b.174 (p.24): the 1874 version has the following note - 'une 3me portée pour Ped.' [a third stave for pedals], and in the orchestra the double basses hold a low D through to b. 181; the same applies to bb.194-201.

Credo, bb.223, 224 (p.43): in both vocal scores RH has gs for *a*s on beats two and four in b.223, but as in b.224; the orchestral score has chords of A minor in the wind, but the organ has C major chords on these beats in *both* bars. The similar passage at bb.3 and 4 of the Credo does not involve the organ and the orchestra has *a*s, not *g*s. The *g*s for the organ are almost certainly an error, but in any case both bars should have the same harmony.

Agnus Dei, b.17 (p.64): the text of the tenor solo here is not usually set to music; the words are spoken by the priest shortly after the Agnus Dei, and are translated in the Roman Missal (1949): 'Lord, I am not worthy that thou shouldst enter beneath my roof, but say only the word, and my soul shall be healed.'

Domine salvum, (p.71): 'The Prayer for the King chanted in some countries after Solemn Mass on Sundays'. (Roman Missal). 'Domine, salvum fac regem nostrum. Et exaudi nos in die, qua invocaverimus te', that is: 'Lord, save our king: And heed us when we call upon thee.' In 1855 for 'regem nostrum' the score has 'Imperatorem nostrum Napoleonem'. Napoleon III was Emperor of France from 1852-1870. The Third Republic was established in 1870, and the 1879 edition has a footnote modifying the text for bb.7-10 to 'Domine salvum fac Rempublicam'. In his 1874 score, published in England, Gounod had 'Reginem nostram Victoriam'. This prayer is offered first by the Church, then by the Army, and finally by the State, the words being the same in each case. The pedalling instructions on pages 71 and 73 can be read as applying to piano or organ, or both.

Michael Pilkington
Old Coulsdon 1999

MESSE SOLENNELLE DE SAINTE CÉCILE

KYRIE

17
p
Ky - ri - e,
p
Ky - ri - e
17
22
p
Ky - ri - e,
Ky - ri -
p
e - le - - i - son,
22

27
-e e - le - - i - son,
Ky - ri - e e -
27
32
SOPRANO SOLO
A
e - le - - i - son, e - le - - i -
TENOR SOLO
e - le - - i - son, e - le - - i -
BASS SOLO
e - le - - i - son, e - le - - i -
32
A
-le - i - son,
32
A

37
-son, e - le - i - son, e - le - i - son.
-son, e - le - i - son, e - le - i - son.
-son, e - le - i - son, e - le - i - son.
37
ppp
Ky - ri-e
ppp
e - le - i - son.
Ky - ri-e e - le - i - son.
Ky - ri-e e - le - i - son.
Ky - ri-e e - le - i - son.
37

42
p
Chri - ste, Chri - ste e - le - i - son, Chri - ste,
Chri - ste, Chri - ste e - le - i - son, Chri - ste,
Chri - ste, Chri - ste e - le - i - son, Chri - ste,
Chri - ste, Chri - ste e - le - i - son, Chri - ste,
42

47
cresc.
Chri - ste e - le - - i - son, Chri - ste, Chri - ste e -
[cresc.]
52
SOPRANO SOLO
TENOR SOLO
BASS SOLO
B
e -
dim.
-le - i - son, e - le - i - son, e - le - i - son,
[dim.]
[p]

57
-le - - i - son, e - le - - i - son, e -
le - - i - son, e - le - - i - son, e -
-le - - i - son, e - le - - i - son, e -
57
ppp
Chri - ste,
ppp
Chri - ste,
ppp
Chri - ste,
ppp
Chri - ste,
57
61
cresc.
dim.
-le - - i - son, e - le - - i - son,
cresc.
dim.
-le - - i - son, e - le - - i - son,
cresc.
dim.
-le - - i - son, e - le - - i - son,
61
p
Chri - ste e -
p
Chri - ste e -
p
Chri - ste e -
p
Chri - ste e -
61
[cresc.]
[dim.]
[p]

65
cresc.
cresc. molto
-le - i - son, e - le - i - son, e - le - - i -
[cresc.]
[cresc. molto]
70
SOPRANO SOLO
TENOR SOLO
BASS SOLO
Chri - - - ste e - le - - i -
f
-son.
[f]
[pp]
[sans Ped]
[poco cresc.]

74
C
- son, Chri - - ste e - le - i - son.
- son, Chri - - ste e - le - i - son.
- son, Chri - - ste e - le - i - son.
74
C
[dim.]
Ped

Chorus
79
SOPRANO
p
pp
Ky - ri - e e - le - - i - son, Ky - ri -
ALTO
p
pp
Ky - ri - e e - le - - i - son, Ky - ri -
TENOR
p
pp
Ky - ri - e e - le - - i - son, Ky - ri -
BASS
p
pp
Ky - ri - e e - le - - i - son, Ky - ri -
79
[p]
[pp]

84
SOPRANO SOLO
Ky - ri - e,
TENOR SOLO
Ky - ri - e,
BASS SOLO
Ky - ri - e,
84
-e e - le - i - son,
-e e - le - i - son,
-e e - le - i - son,
-e e - le - i - son,
84
[sans Ped.]
89
cresc.
Ky - ri - e, Ky - ri - e e - le - i -
dim.
cresc.
Ky - ri - e, Ky - ri - e e - le - i -
dim.
cresc.
Ky - ri - e, Ky - ri - e e - le - i -
dim.
89
[cresc.]
[dim.]
[p]

94
D
-son.
-son.
-son.
Chorus
SOPRANO
ALTO
TENOR
BASS
p
cresc.
Ky - ri - e, Ky - ri - e,
[pp]
[p]
[cresc.]
Ped
99
cresc.
dim.
p
div.
Ky - ri - e e - le - - i - son,
[cresc.]
[dim.]
[p]
[pp]

104
pp
Ky - - ri-e e - le - i - son, Ky - - ri-e e - le - i -
pp
Ky - - ri-e e - le - i - son, Ky - - ri-e e - le - i -
pp
Ky - - ri-e e - le - i - son, Ky - - ri-e e - le - i -
unis.
pp
Ky - - ri-e e - le - i - son, Ky - - ri-e e - le - i -
104
pp
[sans Ped]
111
Più lento
p
-son, Ky - ri-e, Ky - ri-e e - le - i - son.
p
-son, Ky - ri-e, Ky - ri-e e - le - i - son.
div.
p
-son, Ky - ri-e, Ky - ri-e e - le - i - son.
div.
p
-son, Ky - ri-e, Ky - ri-e e - le - i - son.
111
Più lento
p
Ped.

GLORIA IN EXCELSIS

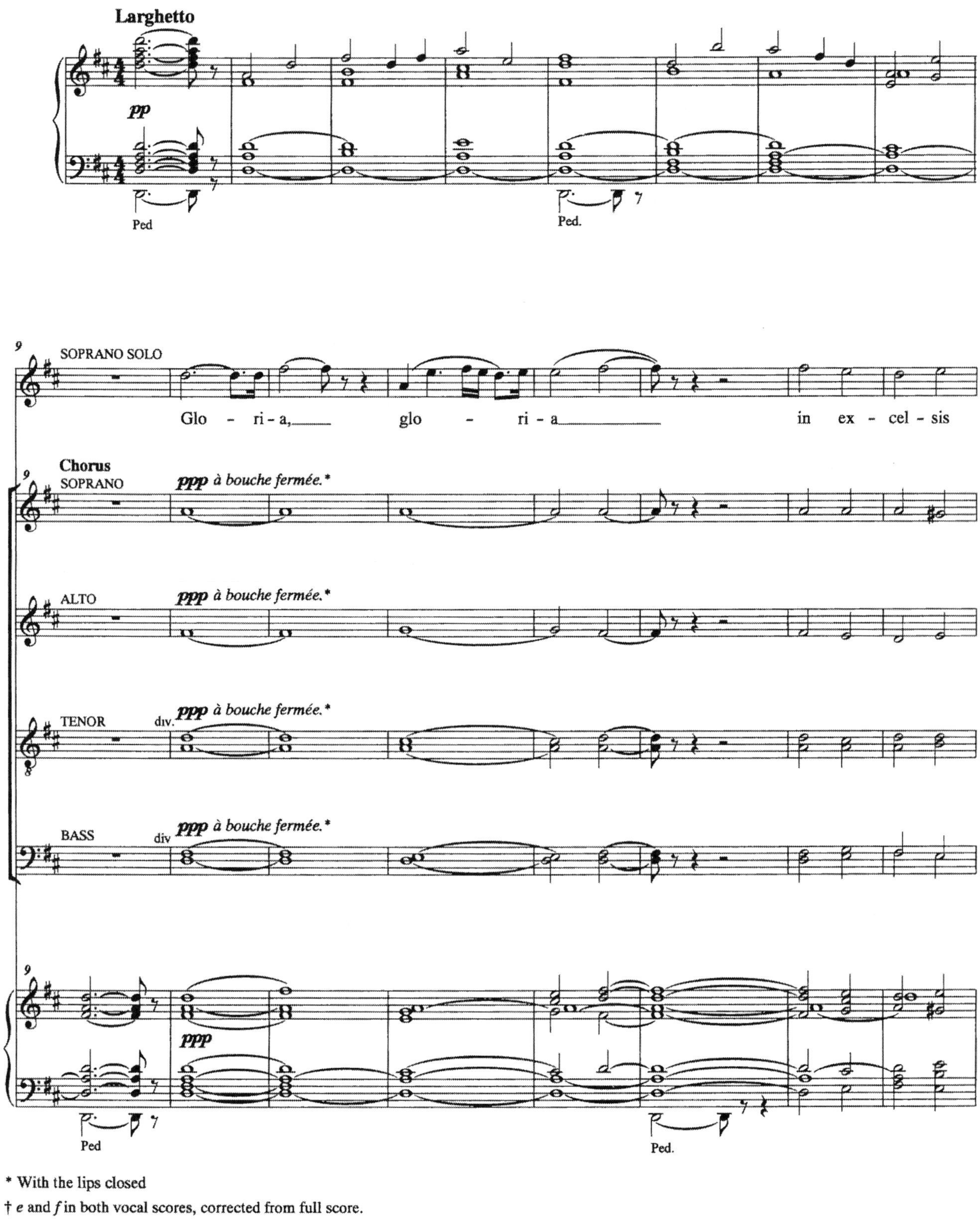

* With the lips closed

† *e* and *f* in both vocal scores, corrected from full score.

17
De - o. Et in ter - ra pax ho - mi - ni - bus bo - næ, bo - næ, bo - næ vo - lun -
17
17
Ped

26
A
- ta - tis.
pp
div.
Glo - ri - a in ex - cel - sis De - o, glo - ri - a in ex - cel - sis.
pp
div
Glo - ri - a in ex - cel - sis De - o, glo - ri - a in ex - cel - sis.
pp
pp
26
A
Ped

Allegro pomposo
35
unis f
Lau - da - mus te. Be - ne - di - ci - mus
Lau - da - mus te. Be - ne - di - ci - mus
Lau - da - mus te. Be - ne - di - ci - mus
Lau - da - mus te. Be - ne - di - ci - mus
Allegro pomposo
Sans Ped
41
te. Lau - da - mus te. Be - ne - di - ci - mus te. A - do -
te. Lau - da - mus te. Be - ne - di - ci - mus te. A - do -
te. Lau - da - mus te. Be - ne - di - ci - mus te. A - do -
te. Lau - da - mus te. Be - ne - di - ci - mus te. A - do -

46
-ra - mus_ te. Glo - ri - fi - ca - mus_ te. A - do - ra - mus
-ra - mus te. Glo - ri - fi - ca - mus te. A - do - ra - mus
div.
-ra - mus_ te. Glo - ri - fi - ca - mus_ te. A - do - ra - mus
div.
-ra - mus te. Glo - ri - fi - ca - mus te. A - do - ra - mus
46
51
SOPRANO SOLO
B
Gra - ti-as, gra - ti-as a - gi-mus
TENOR SOLO
Gra - ti-as, gra - ti-as a - gi-mus
BASS SOLO
Gra - ti-as, gra - ti-as a - gi-mus
51
B
te. Glo - ri - fi - ca - mus te.
te. Glo - ri - fi - ca - mus te.
unis.
te. Glo - ri - fi - ca - mus te.
unis.
te. Glo - ri - fi - ca - mus te.
51
B
dim.
pp

57
cresc.
dim.
ti - bi prop - ter mag - nam glo - ri - am, glo - ri - am tu - am,
cresc.
dim.
ti - bi prop - ter mag - nam glo - ri - am, glo - ri - am tu - am,
cresc.
dim.
ti - bi prop - ter mag - nam glo - ri - am, glo - ri - am tu - am,
57
cresc.
dim.
Chorus
62
SOPRANO
p
cresc.
Gra - ti-as, gra - ti-as a - gi-mus ti - bi prop - ter mag-nam
ALTO
p
cresc.
Gra - ti-as, gra - ti-as a - gi-mus ti - bi prop - ter mag-nam
TENOR
p
cresc.
Gra - ti-as, gra - ti-as a - gi-mus ti - bi prop - ter mag-nam
BASS
p
cresc.
Gra - ti-as, gra - ti-as a - gi-mus ti - bi prop - ter mag-nam
62
p
cresc.

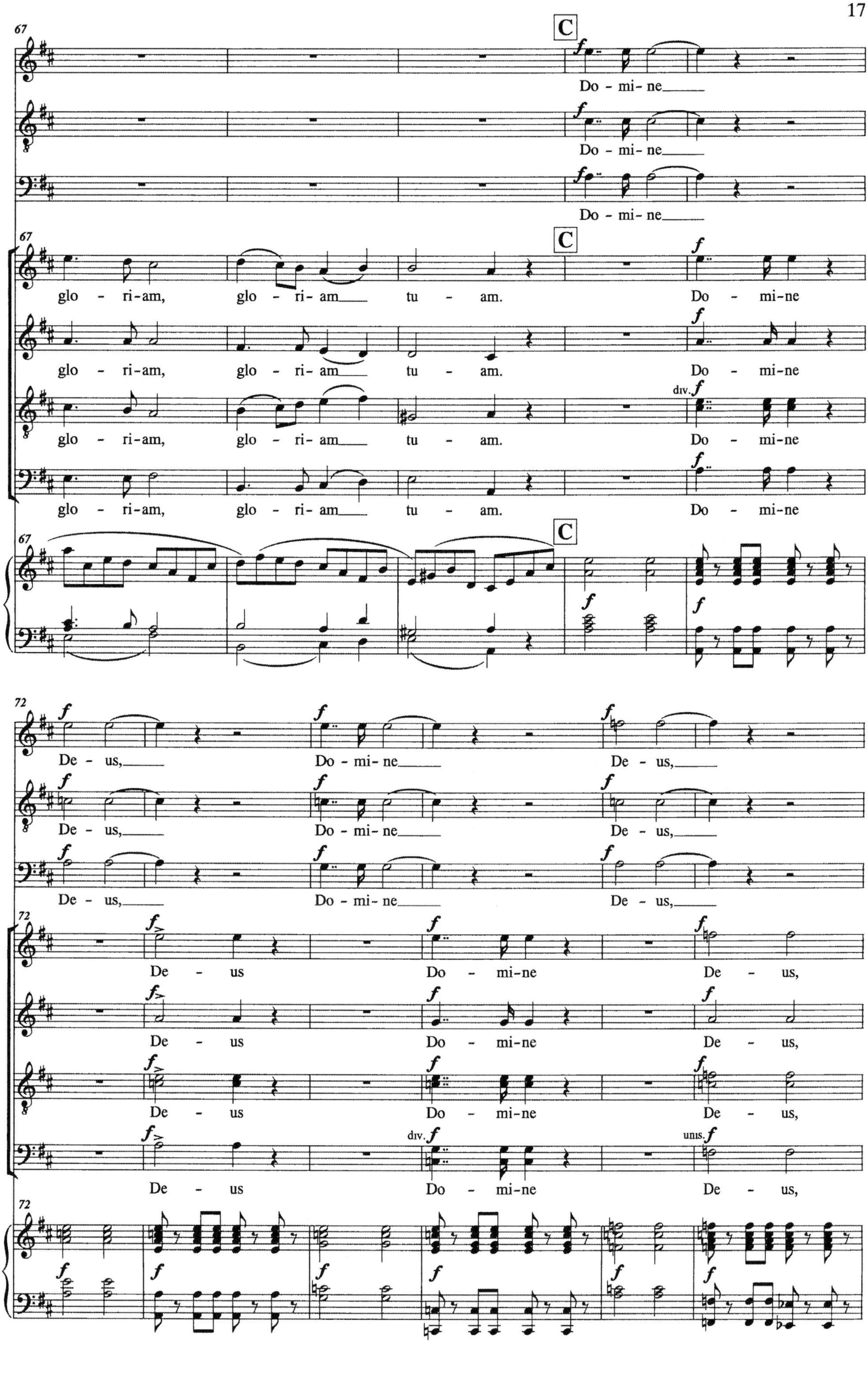
67
C
Do - mi - ne
Do - mi - ne
Do - mi - ne
67
C
glo - ri-am, glo - ri - am tu - am. Do - mi-ne
glo - ri-am, glo - ri - am tu - am. Do - mi-ne
div.
glo - ri-am, glo - ri - am tu - am. Do - mi-ne
glo - ri-am, glo - ri - am tu - am. Do - mi-ne
67
C
72
De - us, Do - mi - ne De - us,
De - us, Do - mi - ne De - us,
De - us, Do - mi - ne De - us,
72
De - us Do - mi-ne De - us,
De - us Do - mi-ne De - us,
De - us Do - mi-ne De - us,
div.
unis.
De - us Do - mi-ne De - us,
72

78
ff
Rex cœ - le - stis, De - us Pa - ter om - ni - po-tens, Pa - ter om - ni - po-tens,
ff
Rex cœ - le - stis, De - us Pa - ter om - ni - po-tens, Pa - ter om - ni - po-tens,
unis. ff
Rex cœ - le - stis, De - us Pa - ter om - ni - po-tens, Pa - ter om - ni - po-tens,
ff
Rex cœ - le - stis, De - us Pa - ter om - ni - po-tens, Pa - ter om - ni - po-tens,
78
f
ff

85
De - us Pa - ter om - ni - po - tens.
De - us Pa - ter om - ni - po - tens.
div.
unis
De - us Pa - ter om - ni - po - tens.
De - us Pa - ter om - ni - po - tens.
85

92
D
Andante
sempre stacc.
p
8vb
marcato la melodia
98
BASS SOLO
Do - mi-ne, Do - mi-ne
[cresc.]
[dim.]
[pp]
dolce
cresc.
102
cresc.
dim.
Fi - li u - ni - ge - ni-te, Je - su Chri - ste,
p
cresc.
106
cresc.
pp
p
Je - su Chri - ste. Do - - mi-ne De - us,
dim.
pp
p
cresc.
110
cresc.
cresc.
A - - gnus De - i, Fi - li-us, fi - li - us

TENOR SOLO
E
Qui tol - lis, qui tol - lis pec - ca - ta
Pa - - tris.
dim.
p
p
mun - di, mi - se - re - re no - bis, mis - se - re - re no - -
Qui
cresc.
dim.
- bis. Su - sci - pe, su - sci - pe
tol - lis, qui tol - lis pec - ca - ta mun - di, su - sci - pe
p
p
SOPRANO SOLO
F
Qui se - des, qui se - des ad dex - te - ram
de - pre - ca - ti - o - nem no - stram. Qui se - des, qui se - des ad dex - te - ram
de - pre - ca - ti - o - nem no - stram. Qui se - des, qui se - des ad dex - te - ram
cresc.
dim.
p

135
Pa - tris, mi - se - re - re__ no - bis, mi - se - re - re__ no - bis, mi - se - re - re,
Pa - tris, mi - se - re - re__ no - bis, mi - se - re - re__ no - bis, mi - se - re - re,
Pa - tris, mi - se - re - re__ no - bis, mi - se - re - re__ no - bis, mi - se - re - re,
135
cresc.
dim.
cresc.
dim.
cresc.
141
G
cresc.
cresc.
mi - se - re - re__ no - bis, mi - se - re - re no - bis, mi - se - re - re,
mi - se - re - re no - bis, mi - se - re - re no - bis, mi - se - re - re,
mi - se - re - re no - bis, mi - se - re - re no - bis, mi - se - re - re,
141
Chorus
SOPRANO
mi - se - re - re no - bis, mi - se - re - re,
ALTO
p
mi - se - re - re no - bis, mi - se - re - re no - bis,
TENOR
div
mi - se - re - re no - bis, mi - se - re - re no - bis,
BASS
div
mi - se - re - re no - bis, mi - se - re - re no - bis,
141
f
dim.
p
p
cresc.

147
f
dim.
p
pp
mi - se - re - re, mi - se - re - re no - bis, Do - mi - ne,
unis
153
Adagio
Allegro Tempo 1
Do - mi - ne Je - su!
Do - mi - ne, Je - su! Quo - ni - am tu so - lus, tu
div
Quo - ni - am tu so - los, tu
[p]

159
so - lus sanc - tus. Quo - ni - am tu so - lus, tu so - lus sanc -
so - lus sanc - tus. Quo - ni - am tu so - lus, tu so - lus sanc -
so - lus sanc - tus. Quo - ni - am tu so - lus, tu so - lus sanc -
so - lus sanc - tus. Quo - ni - am tu so - lus, tu so - lus sanc -
159
f
164
- tus. Tu so - lus Do - mi - nus, tu so - lus Do - mi - nus. Tu
- tus. Tu so - lus Do - mi - nus, tu so - lus Do - mi - nus. Tu
- tus. Tu so - lus Do - mi - nus, tu so - lus Do - mi - nus. Tu
- tus. Tu so - lus Do - mi - nus, tu so - lus Do - mi - nus. Tu
164
f

169
H
p
so - lus, so - lus_ Al - tis - si-mus, Je - su, Je-su Chri - ste, cum Sanc-to
so - lus, so - lus Al - tis - si-mus, Je - su, Je-su Chri - ste, cum_
div
unis
so - lus, so - lus Al - tis - si-mus, Je - su, Je-su Chri - ste, cum Sanc-to
unis.
so - lus, so - lus Al - tis - si-mus, Je - su, Je-su Chri - ste,
f
* Ped.
175
cresc.
Spi - ri - tu, cum Sanc - to Spi - - ri - tu, cum Sanc - to Spi - - ri-
_ Sanc - to Spi - ri - tu, cum_ Sanc - to Spi - ri - tu, cum_ Sanc - to
Spi - ri - tu, cum Sanc - to Spi - ri - tu, cum Sanc - to Spi - ri -
cum Sanc - to Spi - ri - tu,_ cum Sanc - to Spi - ri - tu,_ cum Sanc - to

* See Preface

180
f
-tu, cum Sanc - to Spi - ri - tu in glo - ri - a De - i,
Spi - ri - tu, cum Sanc - to Spi - ri - tu in glo - ri - a De - i,
-tu, cum Sanc - to Spi - ri - tu in glo - ri - a De - i,
Spi - ri - tu, cum Sanc - to Spi - ri - tu in glo - ri - a De - i,
180
[sans Ped.]
185
De - i Pa - tris, in glo - ri - a De - i, De - i
De - i Pa - tris, in glo - ri - a De - i, De - i
De - i Pa - tris, in glo - ri - a De - i, De - i
De - i Pa - tris, in glo - ri - a De - i, De - i
185

190
I
p
Pa - tris, in glo - ri - a De - i Pa - tris, cum Sanc-to
Pa - tris, in glo - ri - a De - i Pa - tris, cum
Pa - tris, in glo - ri - a De - i Pa - tris, cum Sanc-to
div
Pa - tris, in glo - ri - a De - i Pa - tris,
190
I
f p
* [Ped.]
195
cresc.
Spi - ri - tu, cum Sanc - to Spi - ri - tu, cum Sanc - to Spi - ri-
Sanc - to Spi - ri - tu, cum Sanc - to Spi - ri - tu, cum Sanc - to
Spi - ri - tu, cum Sanc - to Spi - ri - tu, cum Sanc - to Spi - ri -
unis
cum Sanc - to Spi - ri - tu, cum Sanc - to Spi - ri - tu, cum Sanc - to
195

* RH note 6: b" in vocal scores, corrected from full score.

210
Pa - tris, in glo - ri - a De - i Pa - tris.
Pa - tris, in glo - ri - a De - i Pa - tris.
Pa - tris, in glo - ri - a De - i Pa - tris.
div
Pa - tris, in glo - ri - a De - i Pa - tris.
210
215
Adagio
ff
A - men, A - men, A - men.
div.
unis
div.
Adagio

CREDO

Moderato molto maestoso
marcato il basso
6
12
Chorus
17
SOPRANO
ff
Cre - do in u-num De - um, Pa - trem om-ni-po -
ALTO
ff
Cre - do in u-num De - um, Pa - trem om-ni-po -
TENOR
ff
Cre - do in u-num De - um, Pa - trem om-ni-po -
BASS
ff
Cre - do in u-num De - um, Pa - trem om-ni-po -
17

23
-ten - tem, fa - cto - rem cœ - li - et ter - - ræ,
-ten - tem, fa - cto - rem cœ - li - et ter - - ræ,
-ten - tem, fa - cto - rem cœ - li - et ter - - ræ,
-ten - tem, fa - cto - rem cœ - li - et ter - - ræ,
23
29
A
vi - si - bi - li - um om - ni - um, et in - vi - si - bi - - li - um.
vi - si - bi - li - um om - ni - um, et in - vi - si - bi - - li - um.
vi - si - bi - li - um om - ni - um, et in - vi - si - bi - - li - um.
vi - si - bi - li - um om - ni - um, et in - vi - si - bi - - li - um.
29
A
ff
34
f
Et in u - num Do - mi - num
f
Et in u - num Do - mi - num
f
Et in u - num Do - mi - num
f
Et in u - num Do - mi - num
34
f

40
f
Je - sum, Je - sum Chri - stum,
f
Fi - li - um,
46
Fi - li - um De - i u - ni - ge - ni - tum.
ff
52
p
Et ex Pa - tre na - tum
cresc.
an - te

58
cresc.
molto
omnia sæcula, ante omnia
63
f
B
ff
sæcula. Deum de Deo,
69
lumen de lumine, Deum verum de

75
De - o ve - ro. Ge - ni - tum, non fac - tum, con - sub - stan - ti -
80
-a - lem Pa - tri: per quem om - ni - a fa - cta sunt.
C
dim.
Ped
86
pp
Qui pro - pter nos ho - - mi - nes, et

* Ce récit du mystère de l'incarnation doit être chanté par les chœurs aussi *piano* que possible, de manière à répondre, par le profond recueillement des voix, a l'impénétrable profondeur du sujet.

This Recitation of the Mystery of the Incarnation ought to be chanted by the choirs as piano *as possible, in order to respond by the profound expression of the voices to the unfathomable depth of the subject.*

102
-na - tus est de Spi - ri - tu Sanc - to
-na - tus est de Spi - ri - tu Sanc - to
-na - tus est de Spi - ri - tu Sanc - to
102
pppp
Et in - car - na - tus est
pppp
Et in - car - na - tus est
pppp
Et in - car - na - tus est
pppp
Et in - car - na - tus est
102
pp
107
Ex Ma - ri - a Vir - gi - ne:
Ex Ma - ri - a Vir - gi - ne:
Ex Ma - ri - a Vir - gi - ne:
107
de Spi - ri - tu Sanc - to
pppp
Ex Ma - ri - a
de Spi - ri - tu Sanc - to
pppp
Ex Ma - ri - a
de Spi - ri - tu Sanc - to
pppp
Ex Ma - ri - a
de Spi - ri - tu Sanc - to
pppp
Ex Ma - ri - a
107
pp
pp

112
Et ho-mo fac-tus est.
Et ho-mo fac-tus est.
Et ho-mo fac-tus est.
112
pppp
Vir - gi-ne:
Et ho-mo fac - tus est.
Vir - gi-ne:
Et ho-mo fac - tus est.
Vir - gi-ne:
Et ho-mo fac - tus est.
Vir - gi-ne:
Et ho-mo fac - tus est.
112
pp
ppp

119
E
SOPRANO SOLO
cresc.
Cru-ci-fix - us e - ti-am pro
TENOR SOLO
Cru-ci-fix - us e - ti-am pro
BASS SOLO
Cru-ci-fix - us e - ti-am pro
p

126
no - bis, pro no - bis sub Pon - ti - o Pi - la - to.
no - bis, pro no - bis sub Pon - ti - o Pi - la - to.
no - bis, pro no - bis sub Pon - ti - o Pi - la - to.
126
Chorus
SOPRANO
ALTO
TENOR
BASS
Cru - ci-
126
dim.
p
p
132
cresc.
dim.
Cru - ci - fix - us e - ti-am pro no -
Cru - ci - fix - us e - ti-am pro no -
Cru - ci - fix - us e - ti-am pro no -
-fix - us e - ti-am pro no -
132
cresc.
cresc.
dim.

* Both vocal scores have ♮ to b, corrected from full score.

158
F Tempo 1
p
cresc.
Et re - sur - rex - it,
p
cresc.
Et re - sur - rex - it,
158
F Tempo 1
163
cresc. molto
Et re - sur - rex - it, re - sur - rex - it
ff
cresc. molto
Et re - sur - rex - it, re - sur - rex - it
ff
cresc.
Et re - sur - rex - it,
cresc. molto
Et re - sur - rex - it, re - sur - rex - it
ff
cresc. molto
Et re - sur - rex - it, re - sur - rex - it
ff
163
p cresc.
molto
ff
168
ter - ti - a di - e, se - cun - dum Scri - ptu - ras.
ter - ti - a di - e, se - cun - dum Scri - ptu - ras.
ter - ti - a di - e, se - cun - dum Scri - ptu - ras.
ter - ti - a di - e, se - cun - dum Scri - ptu - ras.
168

173
fff
Et a - scen - dit in cœ - lum: se - det ad dex - te - ram
179
Pa - tris. Et i - ter - um ven - tu - rus est cum glo - ri - a,
185
G
ju - di - ca - re vi - vos et mor - tu - os: cu - jus

190
re - gni non e - rit fi - nis. Et in Spi - ri - tum
195
Sanc - tum. Do - mi-num, et vi - vi-fi-can - tem:
200
qui ex Pa - tre Fi - li-o - - que pro -

205
H
p
-ce - - dit. Qui cum
dim.
210
Pa - tre et Fi - li-o si - mul a - do -
cresc.
215
-ra - tur et con - glo - ri - fi - ca - tur:
cresc. molto

220
I
fff
qui lo - cu - tus est per pro - phe - tas.
qui lo - cu - tus est per pro - phe - tas.
qui lo - cu - tus est per pro - phe - tas.
qui lo - cu - tus est per pro - phe - tas.
220
I
ff
*
225
Et u - nam sanc - tam ca - tho - li - cam et a - po - sto - li - cam Ec -
Et u - nam sanc - tam ca - tho - li - cam et a - po - sto - li - cam Ec -
Et u - nam sanc - tam ca - tho - li - cam et a - po - sto - li - cam Ec -
Et u - nam sanc - tam ca - tho - li - cam et a - po - sto - li - cam Ec -
225
231
- cle - si - am. Con - fi - te - or u - num bap - tis - ma
- cle - si - am. Con - fi - te - or u - num bap - tis - ma
- cle - si - am. Con - fi - te - or u - num bap - tis - ma
- cle - si - am. Con - fi - te - or u - num bap - tis - ma
231

* see Preface

236
in re - mis - si - o - nem pec - ca - to - - rum.
in re - mis - si - o - nem pec - ca - to - - rum.
in re - mis - si - o - nem pec - ca - to - - rum.
in re - mis - si - o - nem pec - ca - to - - rum.
236
dim. molto
Ped.

J
242
SOPRANO
ALTO
pp
Et ex - pec - to,
TENOR I
pp
Et ex - pec - to re - sur - rec - ti -
TENOR II
pp
Et ex - pec - to re - sur - rec - ti -
BASS I
pp
Et ex - pec - to re - sur - rec - ti - o - nem, ex -
BASS II
pp
Et ex - pec - to re - sur - rec - ti - o - nem, et ex -
242
J
pp

247
pp
Et ex - pec - to re - sur - rec - ti - o - nem mor - tu - o - rum,
ex - pec - to re - sur - rec - ti - o - nem mor - tu - o - rum,
- o - nem, re - sur - rec - ti - o - nem mor - tu - o - rum,
- o - nem, re - sur - rec - ti - o - nem mor - tu - o - rum,
- pec - to re - sur - rec - ti - o - nem mor - tu - o - rum,
pp
- pec - to re - sur - rec - ti - o - nem mot - tu - o - rum, Et ex - pec - to
247
Ped.

253
pp
et ex - pec - to
pp
Et ex - pec - to, ex - pec - to
pp
et ex - pec - to re - sur - rec - ti - o - nem,
pp
Et ex - pec - to re - sur - rec - ti - o - nem,
pp
Et ex - pec - to re - sur - rec - ti - o - nem, ex - pec - to
re - sur - rec - ti - o - nem, et ex - pec - to
253

258
K
S
re - sur - rec - ti - o - nem mor - tu - o - rum.
A
re - sur - rec - ti - o - nem mor - tu - o - rum.
T I
T II
re - sur - rec - ti - o - nem mor - tu - o - rum.
B I
B II
re - sur - rec - ti - o - nem mor - tu - o - rum.
K Harp
pp una corda
Ped
258
pp
262
Et vi - - - - - tam
Et vi - - - - - tam
Et vi - - - - - tam
Et vi - - - - - tam
262

263
ven - - - - - tu - - ri sæ - - - - -
ven - - - - - tu - - ri sæ - - - - -
ven - - - - - tu - - ri sæ - - - - -
ven - - - - - tu - - ri sæ - - - - -
263
265
- - - - - cu - li, et
- - - - - cu - li, et
- - - - - cu - li, et
- - - - - cu - li, et
265

266
vi - - - - - tam ven - - - - -
vi - - - - - tam ven - - - - -
vi - - - - - tam ven - - - - -
vi - - - - - tam ven - - - - -
266
268
- tu - - ri sæ - - - - - - - - - - cu -
- tu - - ri sæ - - - - - - - - - - cu -
- tu - - ri sæ - - - - - - - - - - cu -
- tu - - ri sæ - - - - - - - - - - cu -
268

269
-li.
-li.
-li.
-li.
269
L
271
p
A - - - - men,
p
A - - - - men,
p
A - - - - men,
p
A - - - - men,
L
271

272
pp
A - - - - -
pp
A - - - - -
pp
A - - - - -
pp
A - - - - -
272

274
- men,
- men,
- men,
- men,
cresc
274
Ped.

275
S.
A.
cresc.
A
men.
ff
dim.
277
278
p
pp

INVOCATION

*Offertoire pour Orgue seul**

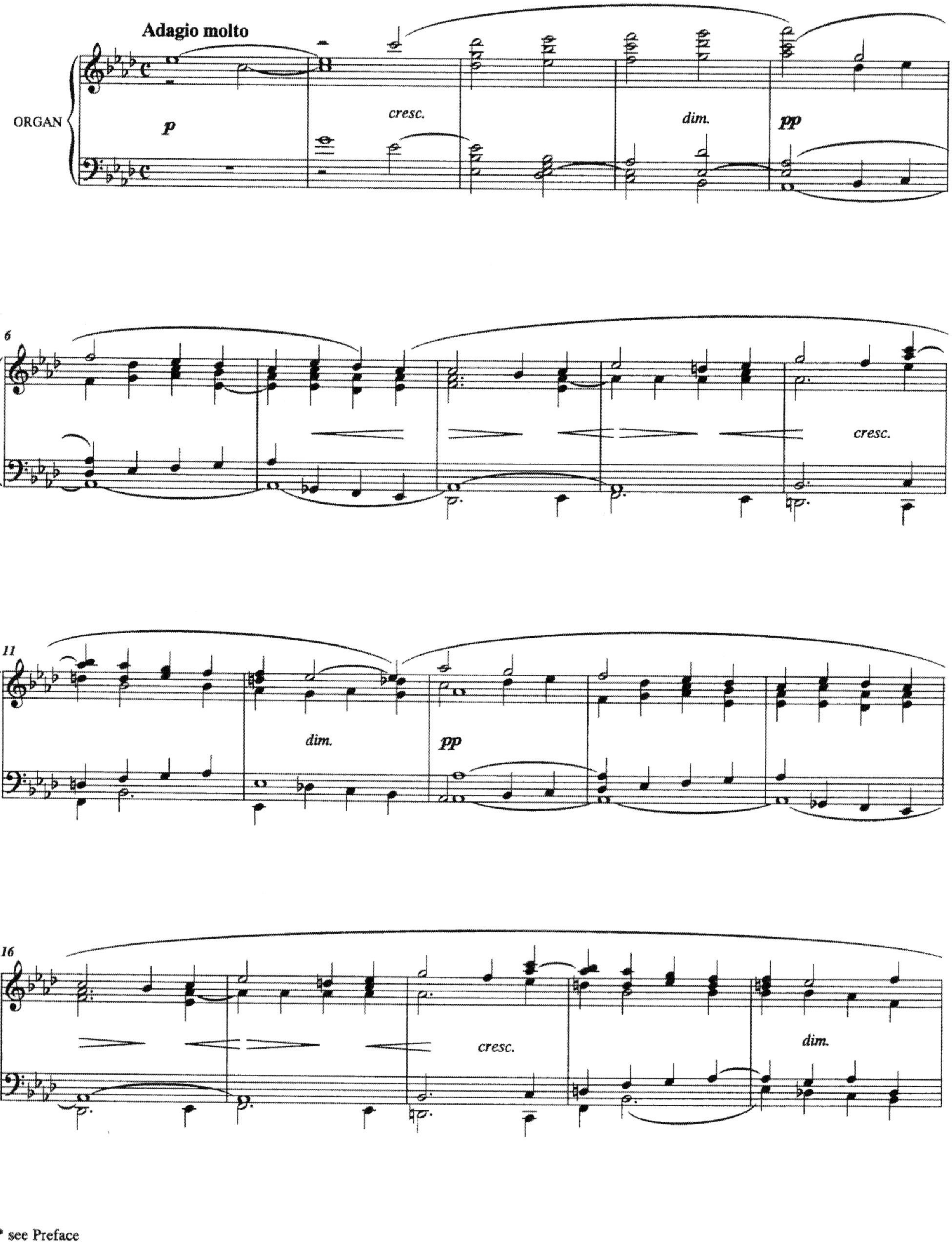

* see Preface

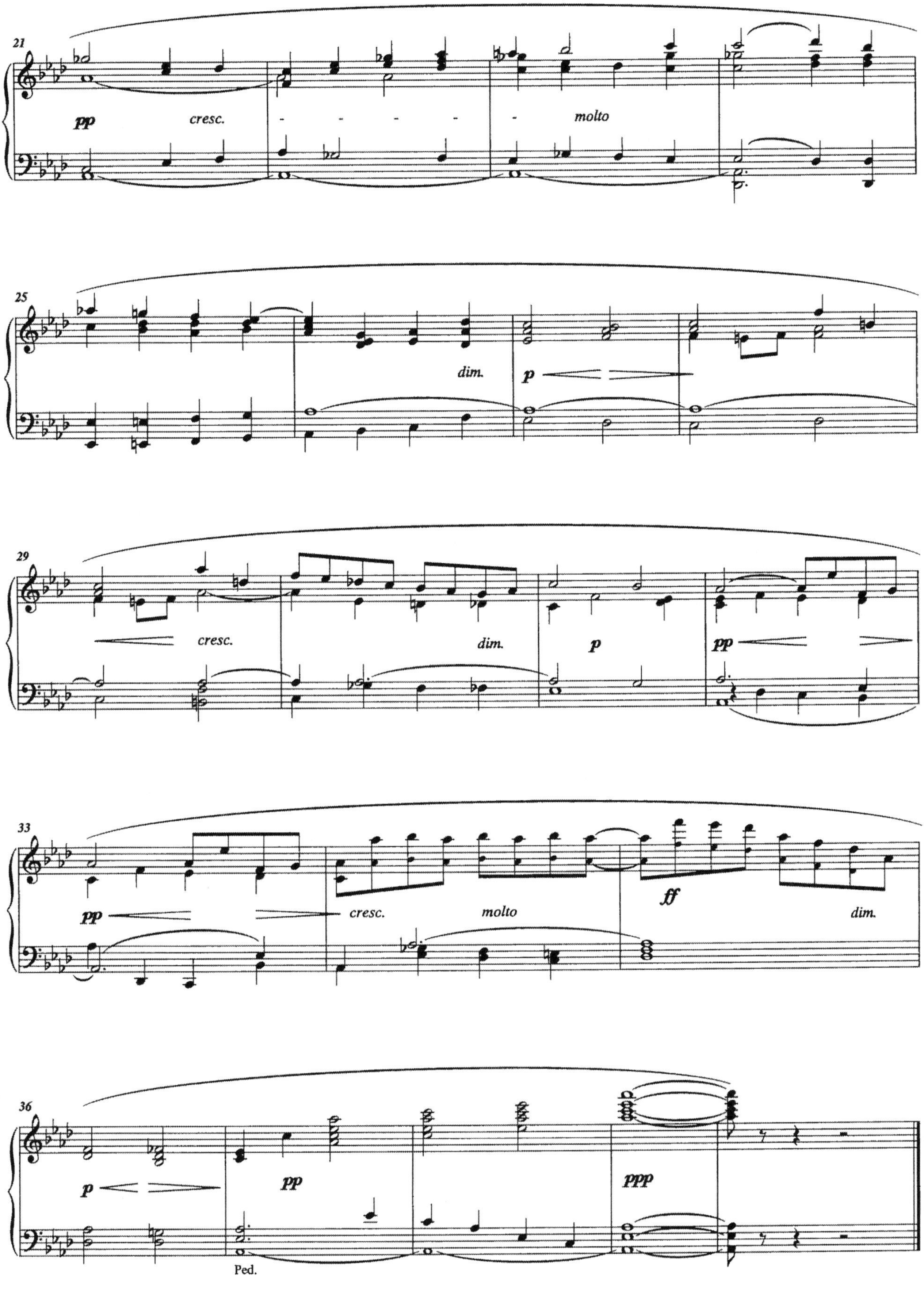
21
pp
cresc.
molto
25
dim.
p
29
cresc.
dim.
p
pp
33
pp
cresc.
molto
ff
dim.
36
p
pp
ppp
Ped.

SANCTUS

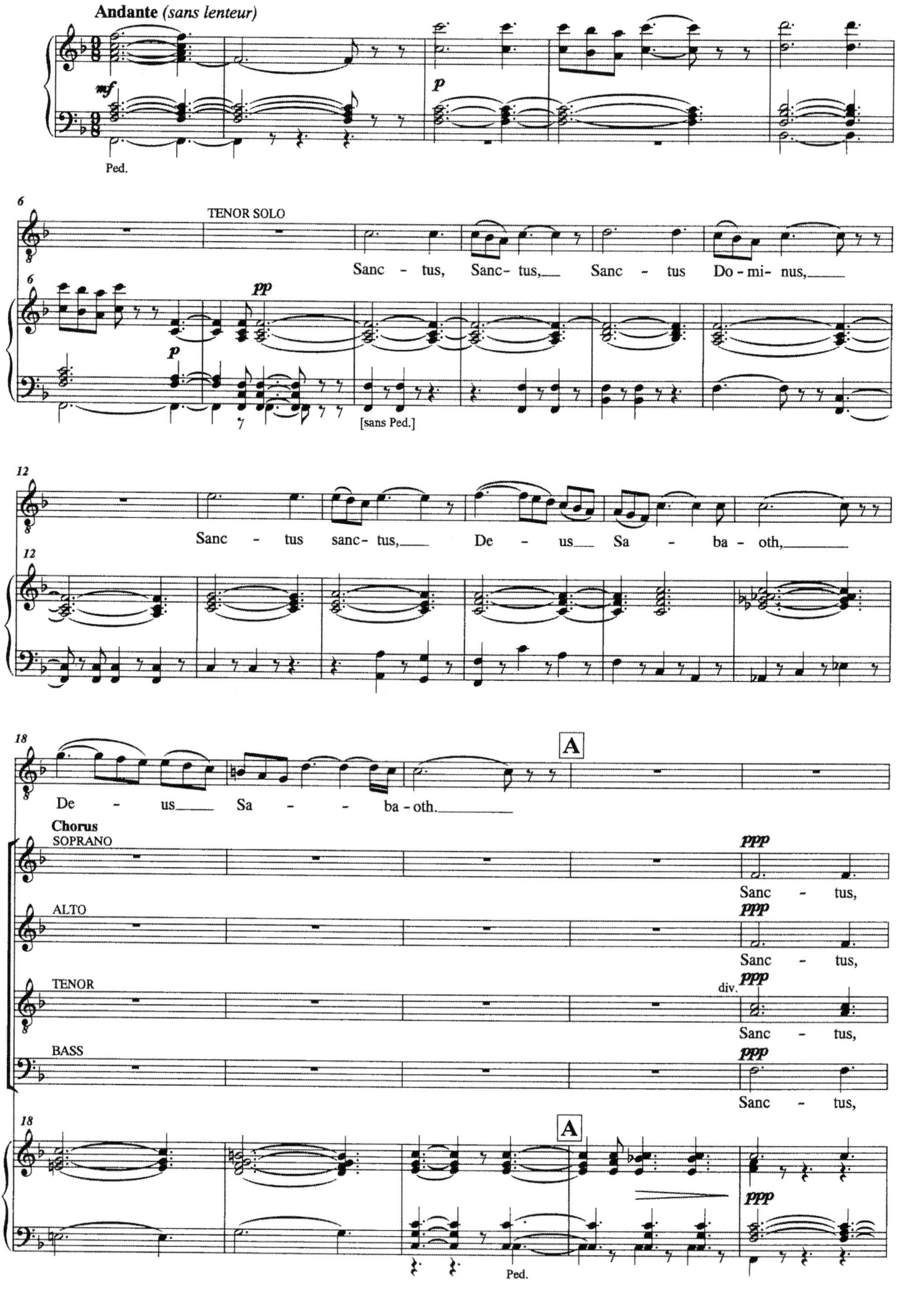
Andante (sans lenteur)
mf
Ped.
p
TENOR SOLO
pp
Sanc - tus, Sanc- tus, Sanc - tus Do - mi- nus,
[sans Ped.]
Sanc - tus sanc- tus, De - us Sa - ba - oth,
De - us Sa - - ba - oth.
A
Chorus
SOPRANO
ppp
Sanc - tus,
ALTO
ppp
Sanc - tus,
TENOR
div.
ppp
Sanc - tus,
BASS
ppp
Sanc - tus,
A
ppp
Ped.

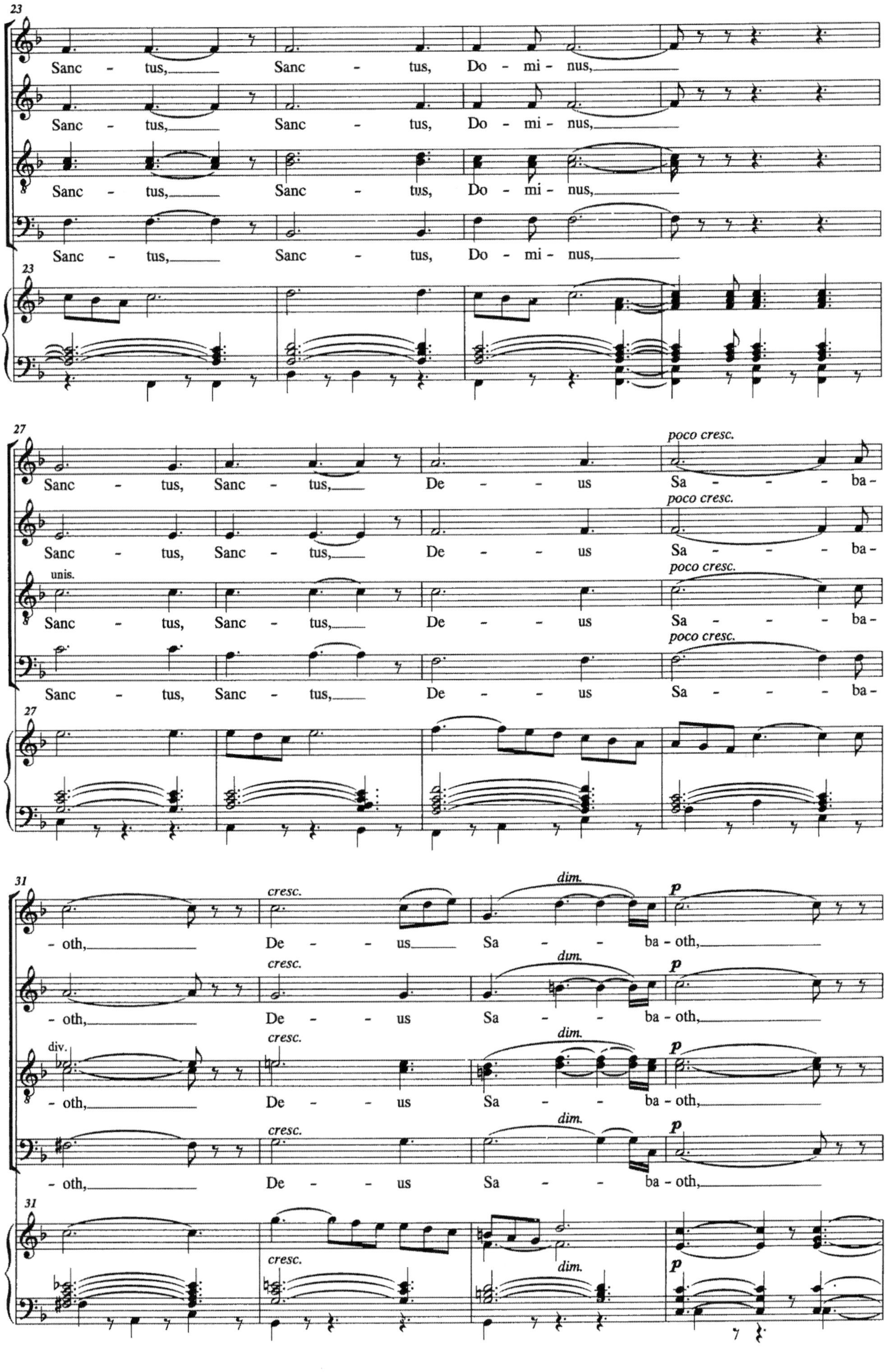
23
Sanc - tus, Sanc - tus, Do - mi - nus,
Sanc - tus, Sanc - tus, Do - mi - nus,
Sanc - tus, Sanc - tus, Do - mi - nus,
Sanc - tus, Sanc - tus, Do - mi - nus,
23
27
Sanc - tus, Sanc - tus, De - us Sa - ba-
Sanc - tus, Sanc - tus, De - us Sa - ba-
unis.
Sanc - tus, Sanc - tus, De - us Sa - ba-
Sanc - tus, Sanc - tus, De - us Sa - ba-
poco cresc.
27
31
- oth, De - us Sa - ba - oth,
- oth, De - us Sa - ba - oth,
div.
- oth, De - us Sa - ba - oth,
- oth, De - us Sa - ba - oth,
cresc.
dim.
p
31

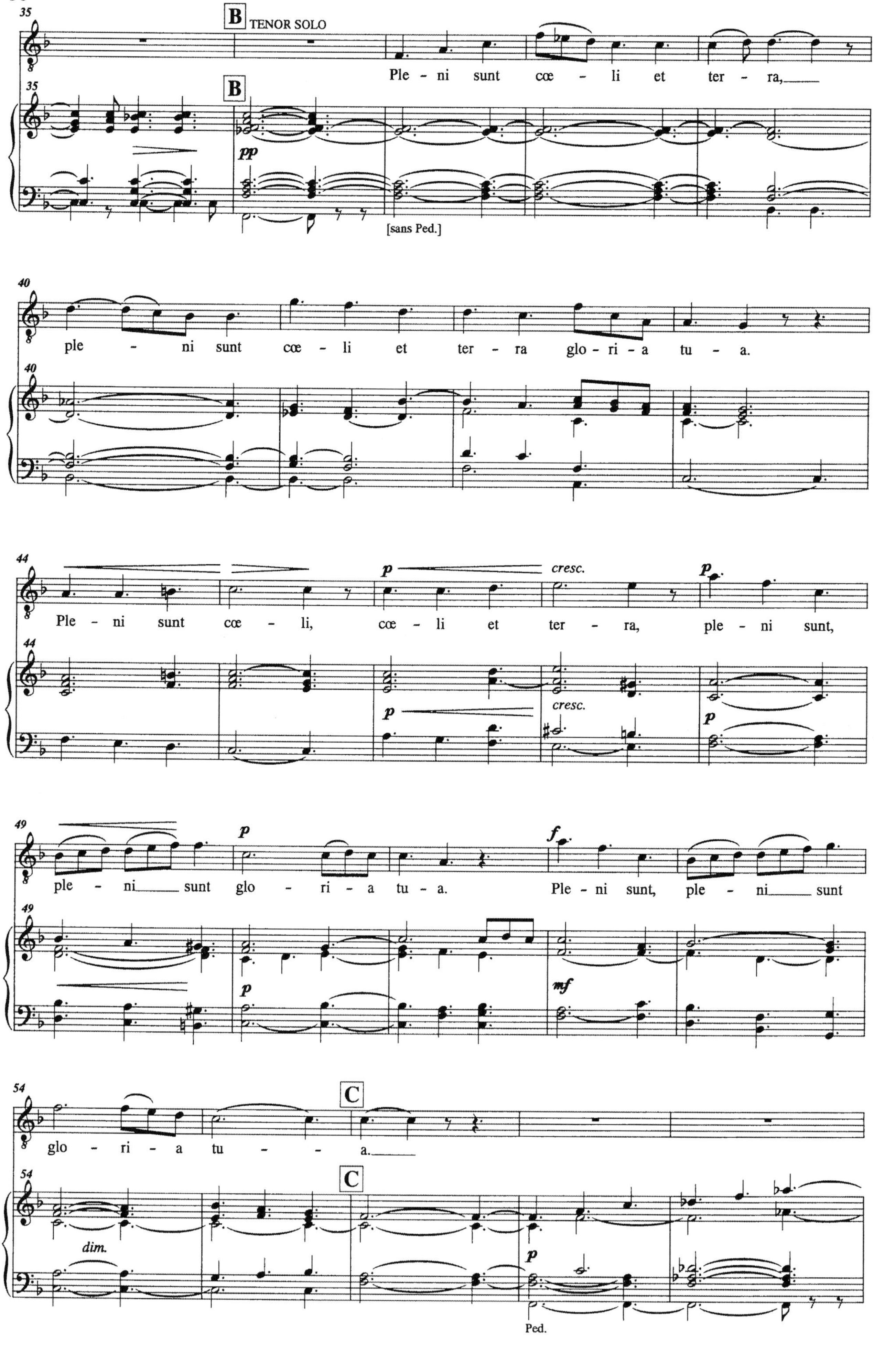
B
TENOR SOLO
Ple - ni sunt cœ - li et ter - ra,
[sans Ped.]
pp
ple - ni sunt cœ - li et ter - ra glo - ri - a tu - a.
Ple - ni sunt cœ - li, cœ - li et ter - ra, ple - ni sunt,
p
cresc.
ple - ni sunt glo - ri - a tu - a. Ple - ni sunt, ple - ni sunt
f
mf
glo - ri - a tu - a.
C
dim.
Ped.

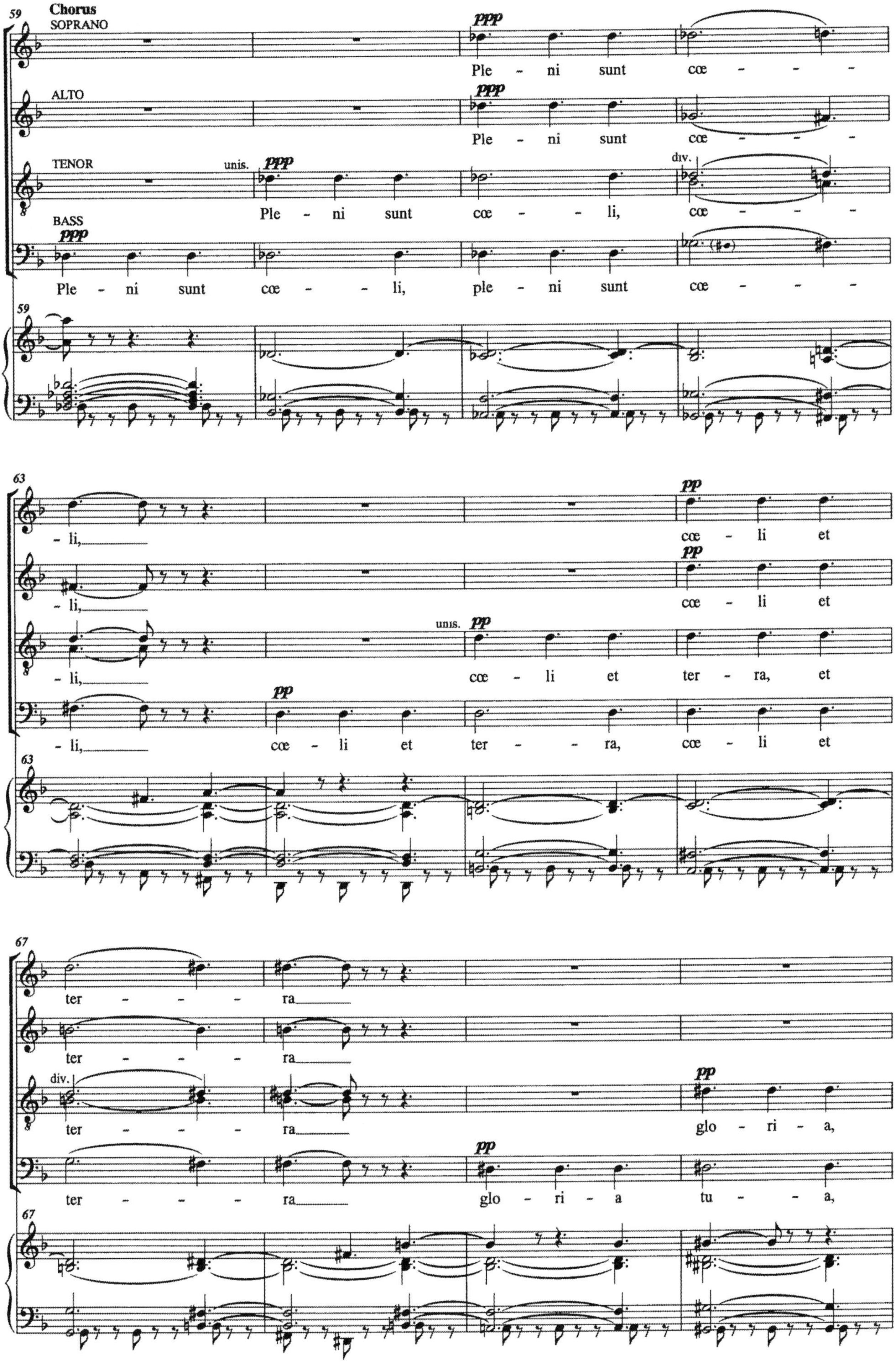
Chorus
SOPRANO
ALTO
TENOR
BASS
unis.
div.
ppp
pp
Ple - ni sunt cœ - - - - li,
cœ - li et ter - - - - ra
Ple - ni sunt cœ - - - - li,
cœ - li et ter - - - - ra
Ple - ni sunt cœ - - li, cœ - - - - li,
cœ - li et ter - ra, et ter - - - - ra
glo - ri - a,
Ple - ni sunt cœ - - li, ple - ni sunt cœ - - - - li,
cœ - li et ter - - ra, cœ - li et ter - - - - ra
glo - ri - a tu - - a,

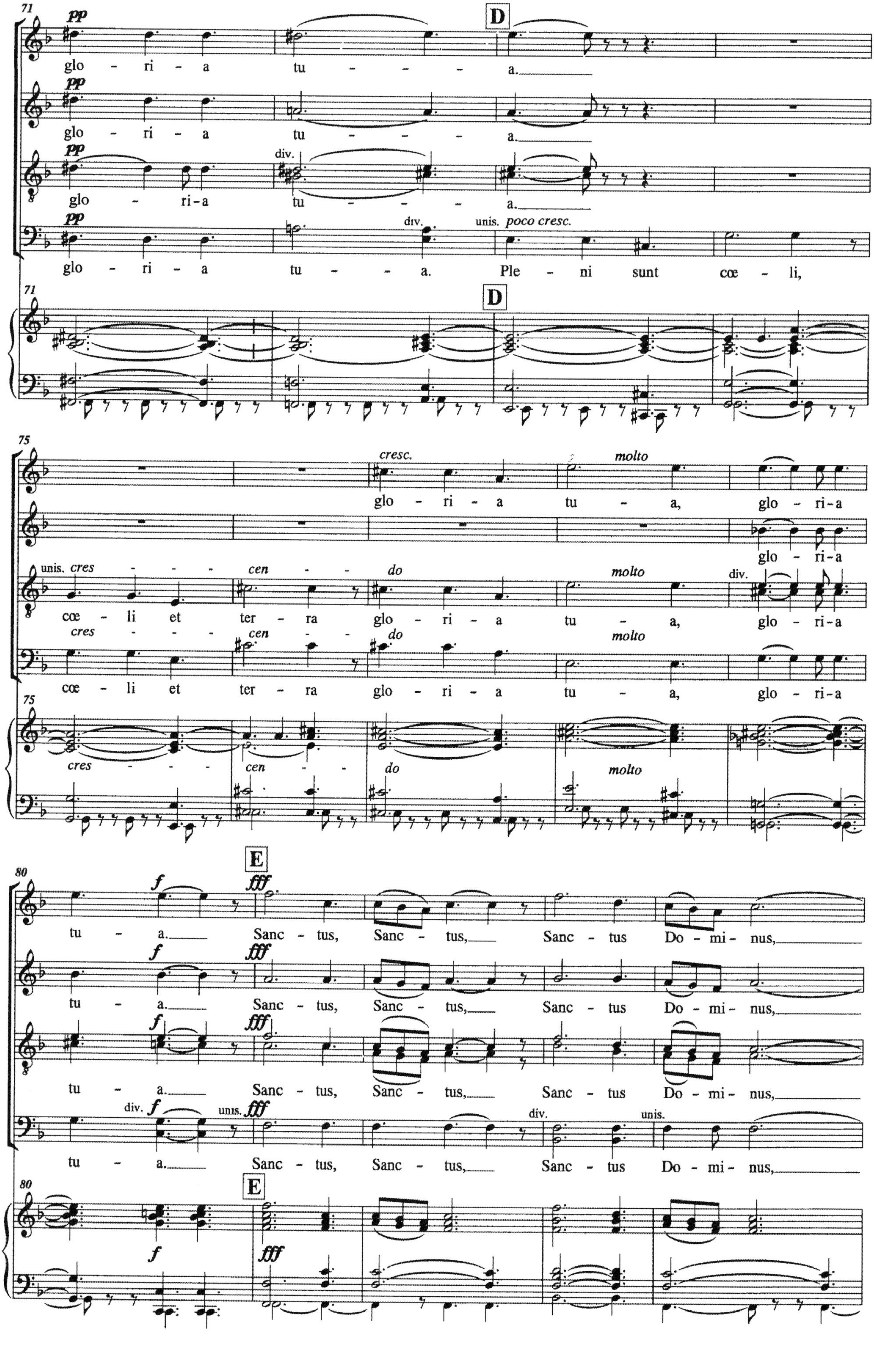
71
D
pp
glo - ri - a tu - - - - a.
pp
glo - ri - a tu - - - - a.
pp
div.
glo - ri-a tu - - - - a.
pp
div. unis. poco cresc.
glo - ri - a tu - - - a. Ple - ni sunt cœ - li,
71
D
75
cresc. molto
glo - ri - a tu - a, glo - ri-a
glo - ri-a
unis. cres - - - cen - - do molto div.
cœ - li et ter - ra glo - ri - a tu - a, glo - ri-a
cres - - - cen - - do molto
cœ - li et ter - ra glo - ri - a tu - a, glo - ri-a
75
cres - - - cen - - do molto
80
E
f fff
tu - a. Sanc - tus, Sanc - tus, Sanc - tus Do - mi - nus,
f fff
tu - a. Sanc - tus, Sanc - tus, Sanc - tus Do - mi - nus,
f fff
tu - a. Sanc - tus, Sanc - tus, Sanc - tus Do - mi - nus,
div. f unis. fff div. unis.
tu - a. Sanc - tus, Sanc - tus, Sanc - tus Do - mi - nus,
80
E
f
fff

85
Sanc - tus, Sanc - tus De - us
89
Sa - ba - oth. Sanc - tus, Sanc - tus,
unis.
93
Sanc - tus Do - mi - nus, Sanc - tus De - us

97
ff
div.
unis.
Sa - - baoth. Ho-san-na, Ho-san-na
101
in excel - - sis.
p
105

BENEDICTUS

Adagio
SOPRANO SOLO
Be-ne-di-ctus qui ve - nit in no - mi-ne Do - mi-ni, in no - mi-ne Do - - - mi-ni.
Adagio
(8 pieds)
pp
cresc.
dim.
p
Chorus
SOPRANO
ALTO
TENOR I
TENOR II
BASS I
BASS II
ppp
Be-ne-di-ctus qui ve - nit in no - mi-ne Do - - mi-ni,
(8 et 16 pieds)
ppp

21
in no - mi - ne Do - - - mi - ni, qui ve - nit in
cresc.
dim.
p
Ped.

28
no - mi - ne Do - mi - ni. Ho - san - na in ex - cel - sis.
ppp
ff
p
pp
f
Ped.

AGNUS DEI

Andante moderato
[sf]
p
sf
p
sf
p
cres - cen - do
dim.
Chorus
SOPRANO
ALTO
TENOR
BASS
p
A - gnus De - i, A - gnus De - i, qui
A - gnus De - i, A - gnus De - i, qui
A - gnus De - i, A - gnus De - i, qui
A - gnus De - i, A - gnus De - i, qui
p
Ped.

10
tol - lis, qui tol - lis pec-ca - ta mun - di: mi - se-re - re,
tol - lis, qui tol - lis pec-ca - ta mun - di: mi - se-re - re,
tol - lis, qui tol - lis pec-ca - ta mun - di: mi - se-re - re,
tol - lis, qui tol - lis pec-ca - ta mun - di: mi - se-re - re,
13
p cresc.
dim.
mi - se-re - re, mi - se-re - re no - bis, mi - se-re - re no -
mi - se-re - re, mi - se-re - re no - bis, mi - se-re - re no -
mi - se-re - re, mi - se-re - re no - bis, mi - se-re - re no -
mi - se-re - re, mi - se-re - re no - bis, mi - se-re - re no -
cresc.
dim.
16
TENOR SOLO
* A
Do - mi-ne, non sum di - gnus ut
p
- bis.
- bis.
- bis.
- bis.
A
p
[sans Ped.]

* see Preface

19
in - tres, ut in - tres sub tec - tum me - - um: sed
22
tan - - tum dic ver - - bo, et sa - na - bi - tur
25
dim.
p
B
a - ni - ma me - - - a.
Chorus
SOPRANO
ALTO
TENOR
BASS
A - gnus De - i,
dim.
Ped.

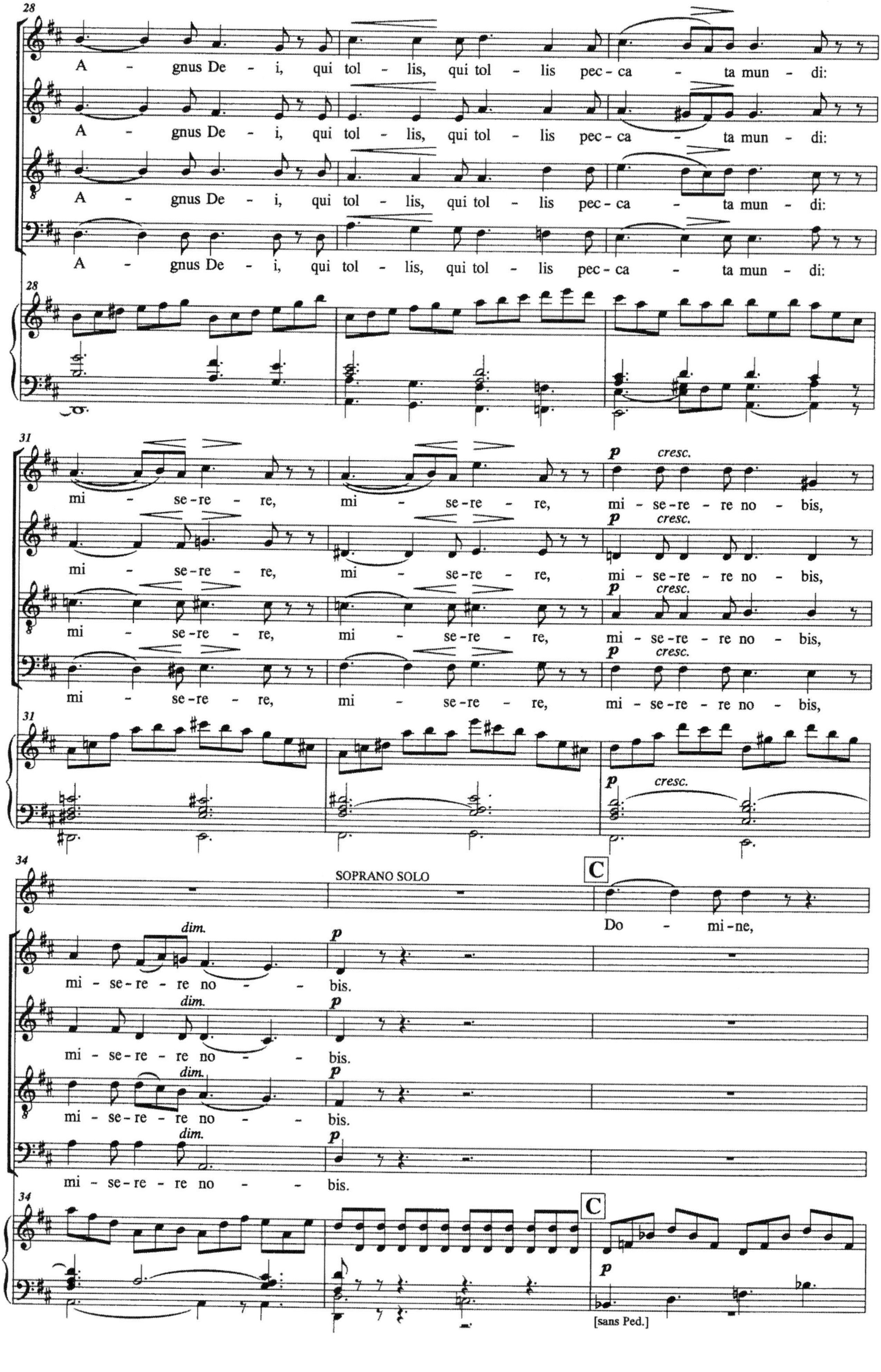
28
A - gnus De - i, qui tol - lis, qui tol - lis pec - ca - ta mun - di:
A - gnus De - i, qui tol - lis, qui tol - lis pec - ca - ta mun - di:
A - gnus De - i, qui tol - lis, qui tol - lis pec - ca - ta mun - di:
A - gnus De - i, qui tol - lis, qui tol - lis pec - ca - ta mun - di:
28
31
p cresc.
mi - se - re - re, mi - se - re - re, mi - se - re - re no - bis,
mi - se - re - re, mi - se - re - re, mi - se - re - re no - bis,
mi - se - re - re, mi - se - re - re, mi - se - re - re no - bis,
mi - se - re - re, mi - se - re - re, mi - se - re - re no - bis,
31
p cresc.
34
SOPRANO SOLO
C
Do - mi - ne,
dim. p
mi - se - re - re no - bis.
mi - se - re - re no - bis.
mi - se - re - re no - bis.
mi - se - re - re no - bis.
34
C
p
[sans Ped.]

37
non sum di – guns ut in – tres, ut in – tres sub te – ctum me – –
40
– um: sed tan – – tum die ver – – bo,
43
et sa – na – bi – tur a – ni – ma me – – – a.
[Ped.]

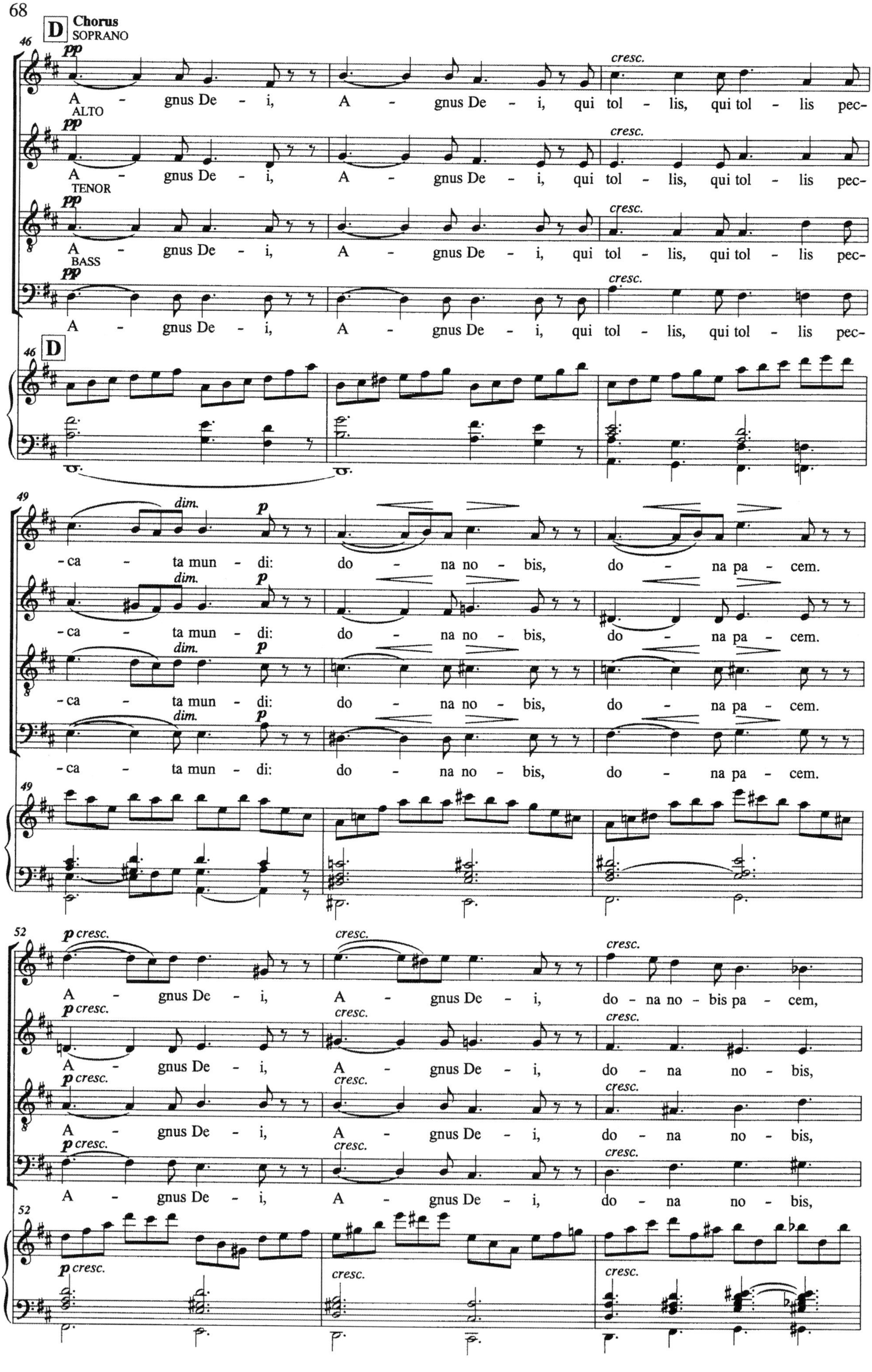
D
Chorus
SOPRANO
ALTO
TENOR
BASS
pp
cresc.
A - gnus De - i, A - gnus De - i, qui tol - lis, qui tol - lis pec-
dim.
p
- ca - ta mun - di: do - na no - bis, do - na pa - cem.
p cresc.
A - gnus De - i, A - gnus De - i, do - na no - bis pa - cem,
A - gnus De - i, A - gnus De - i, do - na no - bis,

55
dim.
E
p
do - na no - bis pa - - cem. A - gnus De - i, A - gnus
58
pp
div.
De - i, do - na no - bis, do - na pa - cem, do - na
61
no - bis pa - - cem, do - na no - bis pa -

64
pp
-cem.
A - - men.
A - - men.
-cem.
A - - men.
A - - men.
-cem.
A - - men.
A - - men.
-cem.
A - - men.
A - - men.
64
67
p cresc. molto
dim.
A - - - - - men.
div.
unis.
67
cresc. molto
dim.
70

*DOMINE SALVUM

Chorus
SOPRANO

1 PRIÈRE DE L'ÉGLISE

* see Preface

2 PRIÈRE DE L'ARMÉE

3 PRIÈRE DE LA NATION

Published by Novello Publishing Limited
Music set by Stave Origination